W9-ATF-082

977.5   34880000401021   5 1695
PAR   Parker, Janice
             Wisconsin

C.1

                                    $16.95
                          BC#34880000401021

DATE DUE	BORROWER'S NAME
05/18/05	Elizo Olayo

977.5   BC#34880000401021 $16.95
PAR   Parker, Janice
           Wisconsin

C.1

              Morrill Math & Science Academy
                 Chicago Public Schools
                  6011 S. Rockwell St.
                   Chicago, IL 60629

WISCONSIN

Janice Parker

Published by Weigl Publishers Inc.
123 South Broad Street, Box 227
Mankato, MN   56002
USA
Web site: http://www.weigl.com
Copyright © 2001 WEIGL PUBLISHERS INC.

Library of Congress Cataloging-in-Publication Data available upon
request from the publisher. Fax: (507) 388-2746 for the attention of the
Publishing Records Department.

ISBN 1-930954-80-8

Printed in the United States of America
1 2 3 4 5 6 7 8 9 10   05 04 03 02 01

Project Coordinators
Rennay Craats
Jennifer Nault
Substantive Editor
Carlotta Lemieux
Copy Editors
Heather Kissock
Michael Lowry
Designers
Warren Clark
Terry Paulhus
Layout
Mark Bizek
Photo Researchers
Mark Bizek
Julie Pearson

Photograph Credits

Every reasonable effort has been made to trace ownership and to obtain
permission to reprint copyright material. The publishers would be
pleased to have any errors or omissions brought to their attention so
that they may be corrected in subsequent printings.

Cover: Fisher (Photo Disk), Cheese (Wisconsin Milk Marketing Board); **Archive
Photos**: page 24; **Cedarburg Chamber of Commerce**: page 20; **Corbis Corporation**:
page 9; **Corel**: pages 4, 6, 11, 28; **Digital Stock**: page 8; **Early Typewriter Collector's
Association**: page 15 (Darryl Rehr); **General Mitchell International Airport**: page 5;
German Fest: page 23; **Green Bay Area Visitor and Convention Bureau**: pages 4, 12,
17, 21, 27; **Minnesota Historical Society**: pages 18, 19; **Milwaukee Symphony
Orchestra**: page 24 (Richard Brodzeller); **Photodisc**: page 26; **Tyler Pickering**: page 23;
Ringling Brothers and Barnum and Bailey Circus: pages 25, 29; **Bob Queen**: pages 6,
7, 10, 15, 16, 20, 25, 27; **Pickin' Up Speed**: page 24; **Lynn Seldon Jr.**: page 15; **State
Historical Society of Wisconsin**: pages 16, 17, 18, 19; **Stoughton Chamber of
Commerce**: page 22 (Beth Bauer); **University of Wisconsin-Madison**: page 7 (Jeff
Miller); **Wisconsin Department of Agriculture, Trade, and Consumer Protection**: page
14; **Wisconsin Division of Tourism**: pages 8, 9, 10, 12, 13, 14 (Ray Miller), 16, 20, 21,
22, 26, 27 (Bob Queen), 28; **Wisconsin Maritime Museum**: page 12; **Wisconsin Milk
Marketing Board**: pages 13, 29; **Wisconsin Secretary of State**: page 5.

CONTENTS

INTRODUCTION

Dairy cattle, ice fishing, and abundant forests can all be found in the state of Wisconsin. The slogan on the license plates of Wisconsin vehicles, "America's Dairyland," displays the state's pride in its strong dairy industry. Most of Wisconsin was carved out by glaciers during the Ice Age, except for the southwestern section. This section, which is largely devoted to dairy farming, is called the Driftless Area because it was untouched by glaciers.

Wisconsin is almost completely surrounded by water. With about 10,000 rivers and streams and more than 15,000 lakes, there is plenty of water within the state as well.

The state of Wisconsin is home to over one million cows that produce about three billion gallons of milk every year.

QUICK FACTS

Wisconsin was the thirtieth state to enter the Union on May 29, 1848.

Wisconsin is nicknamed the Badger State. Early miners in the state often dug homes out of hillsides—like badgers.

The state motto is "Forward."

The state song is "On Wisconsin," written by J. S. Hubbard and Charles D. Rosa.

The name *Wisconsin* comes from the Chippewa word *wees-konsan*, which means "gathering of the water" or "place of the beaver." It refers to the Wisconsin River.

Over two million passengers are served every year by the General Mitchell International Airport.

Getting There

General Mitchell International Airport in Milwaukee is the largest airport in Wisconsin. Sixteen airlines offer about 220 arrivals to the airport each day. For those who enjoy traveling by bus, there is also a Greyhound Terminal in Milwaukee, with buses going to most of the cities and larger towns in the state. Train travelers can take several routes into the state. Highways out of Wisconsin connect to several large cities in the United States. The State Trunk Highway system includes approximately 11,800 miles of roadway and 4,600 bridges. This system makes up about 10 percent of all roads in the state, but it carries 60 percent of all traffic. The main highway, Interstate 94, connects Milwaukee with Chicago to the south.

Location Map

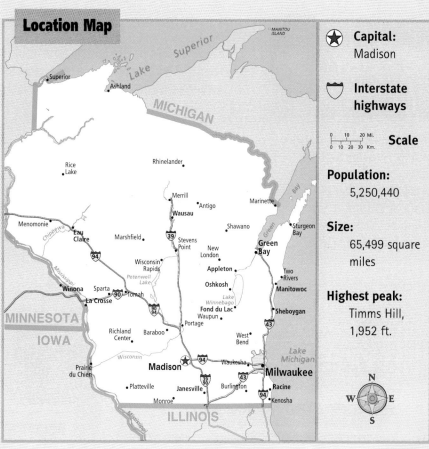

Capital:
Madison

Interstate highways

Scale

Population:
5,250,440

Size:
65,499 square miles

Highest peak:
Timms Hill, 1,952 ft.

Wisconsin is in the north-central portion of the United States. Lake Superior borders it to the north for about 150 miles and Lake Michigan borders it to the east for approximately 425 miles. The state is bordered by Illinois to the south, Michigan to the northeast, and Iowa and Minnesota to the west.

Wisconsin belongs to an area of the United States known as the Midwest. It is among the nation's leading states in agriculture, industry, and natural beauty. Wisconsin is mostly a **rural** state with a strong agricultural base. The larger cities, such as Milwaukee, Madison, Green Bay, and Racine, are urban places with strong roots in history.

QUICK FACTS

The state symbol of peace is the mourning dove.

The state seal was adopted in 1851. It consists of the state coat of arms with the words "Great Seal of the State of Wisconsin" above a line of thirteen stars. The stars represent the original thirteen states in the Union.

Madison lies in the south-central part of Wisconsin. The city was founded by James Duane Doti and Steven T. Mason. It was named after the fourth president of the United States, James Madison.

The state capital of Wisconsin is Madison.

Wisconsin's beautiful scenery and recreation areas attract millions of visitors each year. With over 15,000 lakes, the state draws many people who enjoy fishing, boating, swimming, and other water sports. Skiing, tobogganing, and ice boating are popular winter pastimes in Wisconsin.

The manufacturing industry is a significant part of Wisconsin's economy. The state is one of the nation's main producers of food products, machinery, and paper products.

Wisconsin is considered one of the nation's most **progressive** states. Many social, educational, and political reforms that spread throughout the United States began in Wisconsin.

QUICK FACTS

The area of Wisconsin is 65,499 square miles, including 1,831 square miles of inland water. The state's total area also includes 9,355 square miles of water in Lake Michigan and Lake Superior.

The University of Wisconsin was one of the first in the nation to offer **correspondence courses**. The state had the first **vocational schools** and the first schools for training rural teachers.

Wisconsin is the twenty-second largest state.

The first state to remove the death penalty was Wisconsin.

Wisconsin is almost rectangular in shape except for the Door Peninsula, an 80-mile-long piece of land separating Green Bay from Lake Michigan.

Wisconsin was the first state to pass a law requiring all automobiles brought into the state to have seatbelts.

Wisconsin's long winters make it ideal for winter sports such as skiing and snowboarding.

LAND AND CLIMATE

Wisconsin is made up of two main regions: the Superior Upland and the Central Lowland. Located in the northern part of the state, forests cover much of the Superior Upland. The Central Lowland, in the south, is part of the Interior Plains of the United States. The Central Lowland is divided into two areas: the Lake Plains Area, which is in the eastern half of the region, and the Driftless Area, lying in the western half. Although it has a rocky terrain, most of the land is only moderately hilly.

Wisconsin winters are long and cold, while the summers are short and hot. In northern Wisconsin, temperatures may be lower than –40 °Fahrenheit in the winter and higher than 90 °F during the summer. The coastal areas near Lake Superior and Lake Michigan have milder winters and cooler summers than the interior of the state.

The western and northern uplands get the most rain in the state, with about 30 to 34 inches per year. Lake Michigan's shoreline receives the least **precipitation**—28 inches per year. Rainfall is usually heaviest during the spring and summer. Some areas of Wisconsin receive more than 100 inches of snowfall each winter.

QUICK FACTS

The Fox River is one of the few rivers in the United States that flows north rather than south.

Timms Hill is the state's highest point, with an elevation of 1,952 feet. The lowest point is 581 feet, along the Lake Michigan shoreline.

The Superior Upland is part of the Laurentian Plateau.

Lake Winnebago is the largest lake in the state, with an area of 215 square miles.

The highest temperature ever recorded in Wisconsin was 114 °F at Wisconsin Dells on July 13, 1936. The lowest temperature was –54 °F at Danbury on January 24, 1922.

Thunderstorms, and sometimes tornadoes, are common in spring and summer, especially in the southern section of the state.

Wisconsin has an average of twenty-one tornadoes per year.

NATURAL RESOURCES

Water and soil are Wisconsin's most valuable natural resources. Combined with a long growing season, these resources are key to the success of the dairy and other agricultural industries. The soil in Wisconsin is especially fertile in the southern part of the state.

Commercial fishing has steadily increased in Wisconsin thanks to fish restocking programs.

Although many of the forests in Wisconsin have suffered from **deforestation**, trees are still important to the state. The northern section of the state is the most heavily forested. Including hardwoods and softwoods, about 650 million feet of lumber are produced each year. Hardwoods, such as oak, maple, cottonwood, and aspen make up most of the saw timber. Wisconsin's forests are also important for the tourist and recreational industries.

Wisconsin is rich in non-fuel minerals, such as limestone, sand, gravel, and crushed stone. Copper, lead, and zinc ore are also mined in the state.

Water is another important natural resource. The state's numerous rivers and lakes contain many fish for the commercial fishing industry.

QUICK FACTS

Wisconsin has more than 550 different types of soil.

There are nearly 15 million acres of forests in Wisconsin.

The fish in Lake Michigan were **depleted** after the sea lamprey came to the Great Lakes in the twentieth century. Sea lampreys resemble eels and feed on large fish. A restoration program has helped return many fish, such as salmon, to the lake.

Crushed stone, limestone, construction sand, and gravel make up about 95 percent of the value of all minerals in Wisconsin.

PLANTS AND ANIMALS

Wisconsin was once almost entirely covered by forests. Today, 44 percent of the state is forested. Aspen and birch are the most common trees. The northern part of the state has many hardwoods and **conifers**, including pines and moosewood. Beech trees grow in the far eastern part of the state. In southern Wisconsin, red and white oak, hickory, and maple trees are abundant. Raspberry, chokecherry, blueberry, and beaked hazel shrubs also grow in the state. In the prairie regions, various types of grasses thrive.

Many flowers bloom throughout Wisconsin. The state boasts forty-five different kinds of orchids and twenty different types of violets. Some of Wisconsin's flowers are rare. The dwarf lake iris, which grows in the sandy soil near the Lake Michigan shoreline, is an **endangered** species.

Wisconsin has a large number of freshwater glacial lakes.

QUICK FACTS

The sugar maple is the state tree.

Dogwood, juneberry, poison ivy, and prickly ash bushes are common in the east of Wisconsin.

The state flower is the wood violet.

Badgers live in underground burrows that they build in hillsides. They eat gophers and other agricultural pests.

The forested areas of Wisconsin are home to black bears, white-tailed deer, and chipmunks. The Upland region has red and gray foxes and skunks. Minks, river otters, and muskrats live mainly in Wisconsin's wetland areas. Coyotes roam throughout the state. Bald eagles, wolves, and elk live in some areas of Wisconsin. The state's freshwater streams are home to trout, sturgeon, bass, pike, and muskellunge.

Wisconsin has several different state animals. The badger is the official state animal, while the dairy cow is the state domestic animal. The white-tailed deer is the chosen state wildlife animal.

Eight species of animals and six species of plants are either **threatened** or endangered in Wisconsin. Among Wisconsin's endangered animals are the gray wolf, Karner blue butterfly, piping plover, and Hine's emerald dragonfly. The bald eagle, Dwarf lake iris, and Eastern prairie fringed orchid are among the state's threatened species.

QUICK FACTS

The state fish is the muskellunge (musky).

The honeybee was adopted as the state insect in 1977.

The state bird is the robin.

Coho and Chinook salmon were recently introduced to Lake Michigan and have adapted well.

The largest number of sturgeon per area in the United States is found in Lake Winnebago.

Around 336 bird species are native to Wisconsin.

Black bears are about five feet tall and average about 200 to 300 pounds.

The National Railroad Museum in Green Bay was founded in 1956. It is home to over 70 locomotives and railroad cars.

Tourists in Wisconsin spend more than $5.8 billion per year. The tourist industry supplies more than 177,000 jobs to Wisconsinites.

TOURISM

Tourists from around the world come to Wisconsin to enjoy the impressive scenery and recreational areas. Wisconsin has ten state forests where visitors can camp, picnic, and participate in water sports. The two national forests in the state, Chequamengon National Forest and Nicolet National Forest, are ideal for hiking, camping, and fishing.

The Wisconsin Dells is one of the largest tourist attractions in the Midwest. Visitors can enjoy scenic views of the state's world-famous cliffs and sandstone formations. This area is also known for its water parks. Little Norway, which is 20 miles west of Madison, is an outdoor museum set up like a small Norwegian village. Taliesin, the estate of Wisconsinite and well-known **architect** Frank Lloyd Wright, is another popular attraction.

There are many fascinating museums in Wisconsin. The National Railroad Museum in Green Bay is full of information on the history of railroads and transportation. The Wisconsin Maritime Museum covers the past 100 years of Great Lakes history. The Museum of Woodcarving in Shell Lake contains the largest collection of woodcarvings by one person— Joseph T. Barta. The Barta collection has more than 400 miniature and 100 life-size carvings.

Moored by the Wisconsin Maritime Museum is the U.S.S. *Cobia*, a World War II Navy submarine.

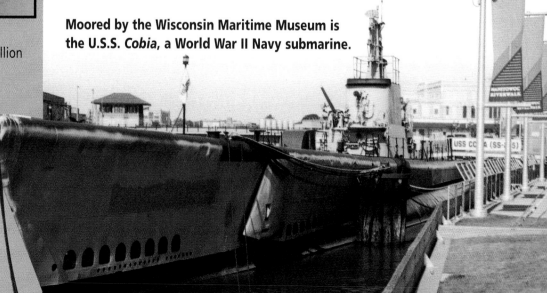

INDUSTRY

Wisconsin's major industries are manufacturing and agriculture, including dairy farming. Wisconsin's reputation as America's dairyland comes from its production of more natural cheese, butter, and milk than any other state in the nation. The dairy industry has been an important part of Wisconsin's economy for many years. In fact, close to half of Wisconsin's 81,000 farms are dairy farms.

The manufacturing industry provides Wisconsin with its major source of state income. Some of the important manufactured products are industrial machinery (especially engines and turbines), food, paper, and metal products, and electronic equipment, including computers.

The forests in the state help support healthy lumber and paper industries.

QUICK FACTS

Wisconsin produces more than 2 billion pounds of cheese each year.

Colby and brick cheese were first made in Wisconsin.

The first ice cream sundae was made in Two Rivers, in 1881. The first malted milk was made in Racine, in 1883.

Nearly 21 million gallons of ice cream are consumed by Wisconsinites each year.

The first hydroelectric power plant in the United States was built at Fox River in 1882.

The Greater Milwaukee area is the state's major industrial center.

Welding is an important process in the manufacturing industry. Welders help make engines, turbines, and other products.

GOODS AND SERVICES

Wisconsin is famous for its cheddar cheese, which is produced in the central and east-central parts of the state. Swiss cheese is produced in the southwest, processed cheese is made near Green Bay, and butter is produced in the west. Most of the malted milk in the United States comes from Wisconsin. The state also produces most of the condensed milk and canned evaporated milk in the nation.

Aside from dairy products, Wisconsin produces food products such as canned fruits and vegetables and malt liquors. Soybeans, potatoes, and hay are also produced in large quantities. Wisconsin has been called the beer capital of the nation because it has a long history of brewing beer.

QUICK FACTS

Wisconsin was the last state to allow the sale of yellow, instead of white, margarine. Until 1967, the state had tried to keep margarine white, so it would not be confused with butter, which was more profitable.

In the early 1900s, Wisconsin produced more lumber than any other state.

Wisconsin has more dairy cows than any other state.

Most cheese in Wisconsin is made in large factories using industrial equipment.

The state grows the most **ginseng,** cranberries, snap beans, beets, and cabbage in the nation.

The paper mills in Wisconsin produce many paper products, including boxes, packaging, and household sanitary supplies, such as toilet paper. There are many metal products produced in the state as well. Some of the metal products include automotive parts, cans for food products, and sheet metal. Automobiles and motorcycles are also made in Wisconsin.

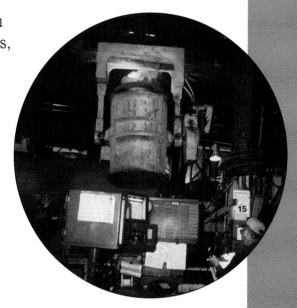

The fur industry, which played a large role in the history of Wisconsin, is still present in the state. Fur farms have replaced most of the trapping, although wild muskrat, raccoon, and mink are still hunted for their fur today.

The fishing industry is small but significant in Wisconsin. Salmon, trout, whitefish, and carp are some of the fish caught commercially in Lake Michigan. Catfish, bullheads, and buffalo fish are caught in the Mississippi River.

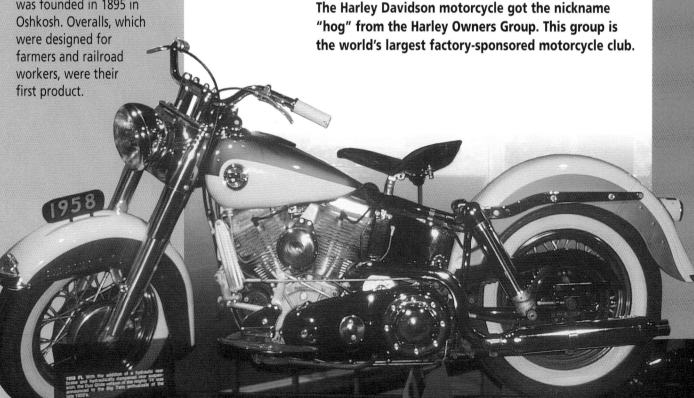

The Harley Davidson motorcycle got the nickname "hog" from the Harley Owners Group. This group is the world's largest factory-sponsored motorcycle club.

FIRST NATIONS

The first Native Peoples to live in the Wisconsin area were Paleo-Indians in about 11,000 BCE. These early peoples were **nomadic** and hunted caribou and other large animals. Another group, who lived in the area around 2000 BCE, may have been the first peoples in North America to work with metal. They made utensils out of copper. Later groups, whom scientists now call the Mound Builders, lived in the area from 1000 BCE to 1000 CE. They built large mounds of earth which were used for ceremonies and burials.

When the first European explorers arrived in the Wisconsin area in the 1600s, there were several different Native Peoples living in the region. The Winnebago, Iowa, and Dakota (Sioux) all spoke Siouan languages. The Menominee, Kickapoo, and Miami spoke Algonquian. In the seventeenth century, other Native American groups entered Wisconsin, including the Ojibwa, also called the Chippewa.

At Wisconsin's Logjam Festival, Native Americans celebrate their culture.

QUICK FACTS

Remains of some of the mounds made by the Mound Builders can be found at many locations in Wisconsin, including Butte des Morts, Azatlan Mound Park, and near Neenah, Lake Mills, and Baraboo.

Today, there are six Native American reservations in Wisconsin: Bad River, Lac Court Oreilles, Lac Du Flambeau, Menomonie, Red Cliff, and Stockbridge.

The Winnebago were nearly wiped out in the 1600s. Diseases carried by early explorers killed more than 80 percent of the people because they had no **immunity** to European diseases.

QUICK FACTS

Father René Menard was the first missionary in Wisconsin. He suddenly disappeared, but years later his clothing was found. The Santee Sioux had been using his clothing as religious artifacts.

The first permanent mission in Wisconsin was founded by Father Claude Allouez in 1665 near Ashland.

Father Jacques Marquette discovered the Fox River portage. This was the small section of land that linked the Fox River, which flows into Lake Michigan, to the Wisconsin River, which flows into the Mississippi.

When Jean Nicolet arrived to greet the Winnebago, he wore Chinese silk robes because he thought he had found the route to Asia. Many fled because he also carried "thunder"—a pistol—in each hand.

EXPLORERS AND MISSIONARIES

Jean Nicolet, a French explorer, may have been the first European to visit Wisconsin. He arrived in the Green Bay area in 1634 while searching for a way to travel by water from the Atlantic Ocean to the Pacific Ocean. French fur trader Médard Chouart and his brother-in-law, Pierre Esprit Radisson, later explored the area around Lake Superior in both 1659 and 1660.

Samuel de Champlain

In 1763, after many wars, France was forced to give Britain all territories east of the Mississippi River, including Wisconsin. In 1783, Britain **ceded** the land to the United States. Wisconsin remained under the unofficial control of the British, who stayed at their military posts until 1796. Between 1800 and 1809, the region was part of the Indiana Territory and then the Illinois Territory. After the end of the War of 1812, Americans began to settle in Wisconsin as the fur trade finally came under their control.

Father Jacques Marquette ministered to the First Nations peoples of Wisconsin, Michigan, and Illinois.

EARLY SETTLERS

Early fur traders, who were among the first settlers of Wisconsin, learned much from the Native Peoples in the area.

In the 1820s, many nearby settlers flocked to Wisconsin because of the lead deposits found in the southwestern area. The population quickly jumped from several hundred to several thousand in just a few years. Most of the early miners came from southern states, such as Tennessee and Kentucky.

The United States signed treaties with the Native Americans in 1833 and 1839. These treaties helped open the land for settlers. New settlers came mostly from areas such as New England and New York. Many of them traveled to Wisconsin across the Great Lakes or through the Erie Canal, which was built in 1825. They settled along the shores of Lake Michigan and became farmers or traders.

QUICK FACTS

The Black Hawk War of 1832 slowed immigration to Wisconsin. The war occurred when the United States tried to prevent Native Americans from returning to their land in Illinois.

In 1800, there were only about 200 settlers—mostly French-speaking—in the Wisconsin area.

The population of Wisconsin grew from 3,000 in 1830 to 11,700 in 1836. Wisconsin's population reached 305,391 in 1850. At that time, more than one-third of the residents were born in other countries.

The first capital of the Wisconsin Territory was Belmont. By 1838, the legislature moved to the new capital of Madison. The original Capitol building in Belmont was restored in 1924.

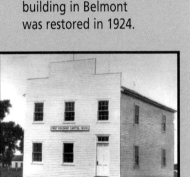

In 1836, the territory of Wisconsin was formed. It included Wisconsin, Iowa, Minnesota, and parts of North and South Dakota. In 1838, the territory was made smaller when the land west of the Mississippi became the Iowa Territory. Many more settlers came to Wisconsin during this period. Most newcomers came from overseas. In 1835, a group of skilled miners came from Cornwall, England, to mine lead in Wisconsin. During the next fifteen years, large numbers of people from Germany, Scotland, Ireland, Wales, Switzerland, and Norway settled in the area.

Lead and zinc ore were the first minerals mined in Wisconsin.

Many early settlers who came to Wisconsin farmed the land.

POPULATION

Wisconsin has a population of about 5,250,000. Approximately two-thirds of the state's population live in urban areas. About one-third of the population live in Wisconsin's largest city, Milwaukee. Still, the population of Milwaukee has recently been decreasing as people move to nearby suburban areas. Besides Milwaukee, Wisconsin has two other cities with populations over 100,000—Madison and Green Bay.

About 26 percent of Wisconsin's population is under eighteen years of age. More than 13 percent are 65 years old or older, which is slightly more than the national average of 12 percent. Nine out of ten citizens are of European heritage, while about 5 percent of the population is African American. Hispanics make up nearly 2 percent of the population. Just over 1 percent of the population is Asian or from the Pacific Islands, and less than 1 percent is Native American.

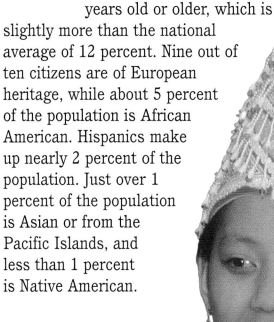

Many different ethnic groups participate in Wisconsin's Triangle Ethnic Festival.

The Capitol building in Madison was designed by George B. Post & Sons. It cost $7.25 million to build.

POLITICS AND GOVERNMENT

Wisconsin has one of the country's oldest state constitutions, which was adopted in 1848 when the state joined the Union. Any **amendments** to the constitution are proposed either by the legislature or a **constitutional convention** and require approval by the majority of voters.

The state government is divided into three bodies: executive, legislative, and judicial. The governor, who is elected for a four-year term, is the head of the executive body. The lieutenant governor, secretary of state, attorney general, and state treasurer are also elected executive officials and serve four-year terms.

The legislature is made up of the Senate and the Assembly. Thirty-three senators are elected to four-year terms. The 99 Assembly representatives are elected to two-year terms.

The judicial body of the government includes all of the state courts. The highest court in Wisconsin is the Supreme Court, which has seven justices elected for ten-year terms. The justice who has served the longest acts as the chief justice. The main trial courts in the state are circuit courts. Any **appeals** go to the Wisconsin Court of Appeals.

The Brown County Courthouse is in downtown Green Bay.

At the *Syttende Mai* festival, there are folk dancing performances by the Stoughton Norwegian Dancers.

QUICK FACTS

About ninety-seven out of every 100 people in Wisconsin were born in the United States.

More than half of the people of Wisconsin are of German descent.

Stoughton has celebrated *Syttende Mai* since 1868, during a peak period of Norwegian immigration to Wisconsin.

CULTURAL GROUPS

Most of the people who settled in Wisconsin came from Europe, especially Germany. People came from Poland, Scandinavia, and England as well.

Within the United States, many newcomers came from New England and the southern states. Early settlers created their own communities and their descendants have continued to practice many of their traditions.

Some ethnic groups in Wisconsin hold annual festivals to celebrate their culture. Each year in Stoughton, Norwegians hold the *Syttende Mai* festival, which means "seventeenth of May." People dress in *Bunads*, which are Norse costumes. They watch and participate in folk dancing and enjoy Norwegian food and music. There are exhibits of traditional Norwegian paintings and needlework. The festival also hosts a contest for children, who compete to draw the ugliest troll.

Perogies can be found at the Polish Fest.

In New Glarus, people of Swiss background hold the William Tell Pageant. German Fest, held annually in Milwaukee, is a three-day celebration of German culture. German musicians and dancers perform, and people sample traditional German food such as schnitzels and strudels. They also get to listen to a Glockenspiel—a German musical instrument.

Milwaukee is also home to Polish Fest, a celebration that is held for three days each June. Polish Fest is an introduction to everything from Poland. There are Polish storytellers, crafts, dance contests, food, and history exhibits. Polish Lowland Sheepdogs are on display, and there is a piano contest that features people playing the music of Polish composer, Frédéric Chopin.

Wisconsin has celebrated the Holiday Folk Fair International since 1943. The fair, which is one of the largest multicultural celebrations in the United States, promotes racial, ethnic, and cultural understanding. It also highlights the contributions that people of various ethnic backgrounds have made to Wisconsin.

The Norway Building at Little Norway houses an impressive and colorful collection of folk objects from both Scandinavia and the United States.

ARTS AND ENTERTAINMENT

Wisconsin is home to many arts groups. Milwaukee has a symphony orchestra, a ballet company, and the Florentine Opera Company. The Milwaukee Art Center is a large museum with an excellent collection of European art from the seventeenth to nineteenth centuries.

One of the best-known painters of the twentieth century, Georgia O'Keefe, was born near Sun Prairie in 1887. She is famous for her paintings of flowers, desert life, and animal bones, which made people look at these objects in new ways.

The film industry brings millions of dollars into Wisconsin, and many big-budget films have been filmed on location in the state. Popular films include *The Blues Brothers*, which was filmed in 1980, and *A Simple Plan*, filmed in 1998.

Wisconsin has many fine bluegrass musicians and is home to The Southern Wisconsin Bluegrass Music Association. Bluegrass music has been described as a pure form of American music. The primary instruments in bluegrass are the fiddle, banjo, accoustic guitar, bass, and mandolin.

QUICK FACTS

Laura Ingalls Wilder, author of the *Little House on the Prairie* book series, was born in Pepin, Wisconsin, in 1867.

Actors Heather Graham, Gene Wilder, Don Ameche, Gary Burghoff, and Spencer Tracy were all born in Wisconsin.

Heather Graham

Talented motion picture director Orson Welles, who made the film *Citizen Kane*, was born in Kenosha.

Bluegrass music is similar to country music, but has a more offbeat rhythm, as well as strong jazz and blues influences.

QUICK FACTS

Milwaukee's Summerfest is the largest music festival in the country, with more than 2,500 performers.

Wisconsin has been nicknamed the "Mother of Circuses" for its role in circus history.

Harry Houdini, who grew up in Appleton, was one of the most famous magicians and escape artists in history.

The first Ringling Brothers Circus was staged in Baraboo in 1884.

The circus business in Wisconsin began more than 150 years ago. In 1847, the E.F. Mabie & Co. Grand Olympic Arena circus moved its winter location from New York to Delevan, Wisconsin. Likewise, the Ringling Brothers Circus had their winter headquarters in Baraboo for thirty-four years until 1918. In 1907, the Ringlings bought another major circus, the Barnum and Bailey Circus. The two circuses were combined in 1919. Today, the Ringling Brothers and Barnum and Bailey Circus still tours the globe, billing itself as the "Greatest Show on Earth."

Many of the barns and buildings used by the Ringling brothers are part of a historical site in Wisconsin. Since the Circus World Museum in Baraboo opened in 1959, more than six million visitors have been to the museum. There, visitors can see over 150 circus wagons on display as well as posters, films, and other objects from circus history.

The Ringling Brothers and Barnum and Bailey Circus founded the Center for Elephant Conservation, which is used as a retirement home for circus elephants.

SPORTS

The Milwaukee Brewers got their name from the city's long association with the brewing industry.

Wisconsin's sports fans have plenty of action to enjoy. There are three professional sports teams in Wisconsin: the Milwaukee Brewers in Major League Baseball, the Green Bay Packers in the National Football League (NFL), and the Milwaukee Bucks in the National Basketball Association (NBA). The Milwaukee Bucks entered the NBA in the 1968–1969 season. They won the NBA crown in their third season. Basketball legend Kareem Abdul-Jabbar played center for the team.

The Green Bay Packers were one of the founding teams of the NFL. The Packers have won twelve championships—more than any other team in the history of the NFL. Four Packer players have won the Heisman Trophy for best quarterback: Bruce Smith in 1941, Paul Hornung in 1961, Ty Detmer in 1990, and Desmond Howard in 1991.

The Green Bay Packers call Lambeau Field home. The stadium can hold over 60,000 fans.

QUICK FACTS

The largest cross-country ski race in the United States is held in Wisconsin. The American Birkebeiner is held between Hayward and Cable.

There are about 40 downhill ski areas in Wisconsin.

In 1978, the first World Cup cross-country ski races were held on the Telemark Trails in Wisconsin.

Windsurfing is a popular water sport that combines sailing and surfing.

Lake Michigan and many inland lakes in Wisconsin are popular locations for water sports such as sailing, boating, and water-skiing. Boat races, called regattas, are held on Lake Winnebago each year. Regattas have been held there since the early 1900s. In the winter, snowmobiling, iceboating, sledding, downhill skiing, cross-country skiing, and ice skating are popular sports for Wisconsinites and tourists.

QUICK FACTS

Wisconsin native and speed skater Eric Heiden won five Olympic gold medals in 1980.

The first season for the Milwaukee Brewers was in 1970.

The Green Bay Packers have their own Hall of Fame in Green Bay.

Hunting and fishing are popular sports for some Wisconsin residents and tourists.

The word hockey comes from the French word *hoquet* which means "shepherd's stick."

Brain Teasers

1

TRUE OR FALSE?

Wisconsin's largest inland lake is Lake Michigan.

Answer: False. Lake Winnebago is the largest inland lake in Wisconsin.

2

Which one of the following slogans appears on Wisconsin license plates?

a) Forward
b) America's Dairyland
c) The Badger State
d) Butter Land

Answer: b) The slogan "America's Dairyland" appears on Wisconsin license plates.

3

Most of the distinctive landforms in Wisconsin were caused by which of the following:

a) earthquakes
b) Lake Michigan
c) wind
d) glaciers

Answer: d) glaciers

4

TRUE OR FALSE?

The state animal of Wisconsin is the mule deer.

Answer: False. The state animal is the badger. The state wildlife animal is the white-tailed deer.

5

Which of the following famous people were born in Wisconsin?

a) Golda Meir, past prime minister of Israel
b) John F. Kennedy, past president of the United States
c) Liberace, pianist
d) Harrison Ford, actor
e) Douglas MacArthur, General
f) Thornton Wilder, Pulitzer Prize-winning author
g) Harry Houdini, magician

Answer: c), d), f), g). Golda Meir was born in Russia in 1898. She moved to Milwaukee with her family in 1906. General MacArthur was born in Little Rock, Arkansas, and John F. Kennedy was born in Brookline, Massachusetts.

6

What percentage of the nation's cheese is produced in Wisconsin?

a) 10 percent
b) 30 percent
c) 50 percent
d) 70 percent

Answer:
b) 30% of the nation's cheese is produced in Wisconsin.

7

The Ringling Bros. Circus was founded in Baraboo, Wisconsin, in what year?

a) 1964
b) 1854
c) 1884
d) 1924

Answer: c) 1884

8

Place the following cities in order of highest to lowest population according to 1996 population estimates:

Green Bay   Eau Claire
Oshkosh   West Allis
Appleton   Kenosha
Milwaukee   Madison
Racine   Waukesha

Answer:

1. Milwaukee   6. Appleton
2. Madison   7. West Allis
3. Green Bay   8. Oshkosh
4. Kenosha   9. Waukesha
5. Racine   10. Eau Claire

FOR MORE INFORMATION

Books

Bock, Judy and Rachel Kranz. *Scholastic Encyclopedia of the United States*. New York: Scholastic, 1997.

Gall, Timothy and Susan Gall, eds. *Junior Worldmark Encyclopedia of the States*. Detroit: UXL, 1996.

Hicks, Roger. *The Big Book of America*. Philadelphia: Courage Books, 1994.

Web sites

You can also go online and have a look at the following Web sites:

Wisconsin.com
http://www.wisconsin.com

Just For Kids: Wisconsin State Senate
http://www.legis.state.wi.us/senate/scc/kids/index.htm

State of Wisconsin
http://badger.state.wi.us

Some Web sites stay current longer than others. To find other Wisconsin Web sites, enter search terms, such as "Wisconsin" or "Green Bay Packers," or any other topic you want to research.

GLOSSARY

amendment: the formal change of, or addition to, a bill or constitution

appeal: a case transferred to a higher authority for a decision

architect: a person who designs buildings and supervises their construction

ceded: gave up possession of an object or piece of land

conifer: a type of tree or shrub that holds its seeds in cones

constitutional convention: a meeting of American leaders to decide upon possible changes to the constitution

cornucopia: a horn full of food and drink, meant to symbolize an endless supply

correspondence courses: distance education classes or studies done through written mail

deforestation: to cut down and clear away trees

depleted: run out

endangered: at risk of disappearing or becoming extinct

ginseng: a plant used for its medicinal properties

immunity: protected from disease

nomadic: characteristics of a people who have no permanent home

precipitation: any form of moisture that falls from the atmosphere—rain, snow, hail

progressive: striving toward better conditions in society and government

rural: relating to the country or farming

threatened: at risk of becoming endangered

vocational schools: schools that concentrate on the learning of a trade

INDEX